Simon Morley is thirty-four and has worked for many years as a comedy promoter. **David 'Friendy' Friend** is thirty-one and studied computing at Southern Cross University. They met in a pub, when David approached Simon and said, 'I believe you can do dick tricks.' They both originate from Melbourne, Australia.

PUPPETRY OF THE PENIS

Simon Morley & David Friend

RANDOM HOUSE AUSTRALIA

Random House Australia Pty Ltd
20 Alfred Street, Milsons Point, NSW 2061
http://www.randomhouse.com.au

Sydney   New York   Toronto
London   Auckland   Johannesburg

First published in Great Britain by Bantam Press 2000
This Random House Australia edition first published 2001

National Library of Australia

Cataloguing-in-Publication Entry

Morley, Simon.
Puppetry of the penis.

ISBN 1 74051 067 4.

1. Penis - Humor. 2. Penis - Miscellanea. 3. Australian wit and humor.
4. Generative organs, Male - In art.

I. Friend, David. II. Title.

611.64

Photographs © Johnny Ring 2000
Illustrations © Fred Negro 2000

Typeset in Sabon 11/14pt

Printed by australian book connection

10 9 8 7 6 5 4 3 2

To our mothers, Marie and Mally,
and mothers of the world

NOTE FROM THE PUBLISHERS

While we are of the strong opinion that it is the inalienable right of each and every man to perform dick tricks in the comfort and privacy of his own home – though not in public unless requested to do so – and that with due care and attention these tricks can be replicated by almost any man, we must emphasize that Simon and David are experienced professionals using highly calibrated, top-of-the-range equipment, and that you attempt their magnificent art form at your own risk.

Seriously, guys, these two men are experts in their field and have practiced their genital manipulation for years, so be extremely careful when imitating them.

INTRODUCTION

We women have always suspected that blokes are a lower life form. I mean, men think sitting on the toilet is a leisure activity. They play air guitar. They fiddle with the fridge thermostat, 'just for fun'. They think 'sex drive' means doing it in the car – no doubt because the sign on the rear-view mirror says, 'Objects in the mirror may appear larger than they are'. They have pet names for their penises – I don't know about you, but I am yet to be informally introduced to a vagina.

Well, *Puppetry of the Penis* confirms these suspicions. We now have categorical proof that yes, if men were any more moronic we'd have to water them once a week.

WARNING: the following craft ideas are for amateurs. Do try this in your own home.

Kathy Lette

A MESSAGE FROM
THE GRANDMASTER

For many centuries the ancient art of genital origami has been handed down from generation to generation by my people in the village of Lonshlong in South-east Asia. As a boy, I recall sitting on my father's knee as he explained the history of genital origami to me. He told me it was derived from a martial art more commonly known as cockfighting, and was then used as a form of self-defence in our province. However, following a period of peace and tranquillity in our village, this art form has been transformed into a force for good.

Genital origami is now used to promote happiness and laughter. In the West there is much shame attached to the penis, but to my people it is an object of delight. We believe there is too much sadness in the West, so it has been decided by my elders that I should present this art form to the world.

As my friend his Holiness the Dalai Lama says, 'The first step towards wisdom is mastering the obvious, and the more you experiment the more you learn, the more you learn the more you create.' I wish you many happy hours of experimentation, but remember, be guided by realism, moderation and patience.

Grandmaster Chow Kai-Seng

THE GRANDMASTER
INTRODUCES HIS GRASSHOPPERS

SIMON

On my pilgrimage to Australia, the largest continent near to my beloved home, I met Simon, who I call Wan Lon Dong. I was impressed to find a grasshopper who was already experimenting with a crude form of genital origami. He practises this in places you call nightclub toilets, sporting changing rooms and at selected family gatherings. My grandfather always told me, 'The more clay the sculptor has to work with, the more he can create.' Wan Lon Dong has much clay. I have taught him wisdom, serenity and the joy of bringing laughter to others.

FRIENDY

In Australia I also find Friendy, who I call Hee Hung Tu. I discover Friendy from reputation and strong word of mouth. He makes a most enthusiastic grasshopper since he started experimenting in the bath as a small child. He developed his craft through much drink at university.

THE GRANDMASTER
EDUCATES HIS GRASSHOPPERS

HISTORY OF
PUPPETRY OF THE PENIS

Puppetry of the Penis was conceived by Simon Morley in 1996 as the title of a classy, highbrow art calendar, containing twelve of his favourite dick tricks. Simon's youngest brother had shown him his first dick trick, 'Hamburger'. The sibling rivalry between him and his three brothers resulted in the evolution of a healthy repertoire of genital tricks.

It was on New Year's Eve in 1997, with a garage full of calendars to shift and burgeoning requests for private live shows, that he finally decided to unleash his talents on the world.

The natural choice of partner was Friendy, whose reputation as the perfect man to entertain parties and hen nights was quickly growing. After studying for years at university near Byron Bay, he had returned to Melbourne with his own particular collection of genital tricks, and a partnership with the other dick-tricker on the circuit was a natural progression that resulted in Friendy's becoming one half of *Puppetry of the Penis*.

After a hit first season at the 1998 Melbourne Comedy Festival, Simon and Friendy embarked on a national tour, circumnavigating Australia. This took eight months, covered 20,000 kilometres and was captured in all its glory in the documentary *Tackle Happy*.

Subsequent sell-out tours in Sydney and Melbourne resulted in the boys taking their wares to the Edinburgh International Fringe Festival, where they were humbled by yet another sell-out season. West End producers realized the full potential of the show after attending a performance where a woman sitting next to them wet her pants laughing. A deal was made on the spot, and *Puppetry of the Penis* was on its way to the West End.

The rest will be history.

THE TOOLS OF THE TRADE

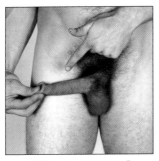

THE PENIS

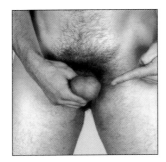

THE TESTICLES

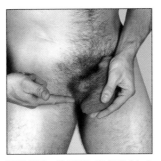

THE SCROTUM

BECOMING COMFORTABLE
WITH YOUR NUDITY

A complete lack of shame is an essential quality for a dick-tricker. You must be comfortable with your body and happy to display it, as you will need to be naked from shoulders to ankles while performing – clothing will restrict your movement.

SOME WAYS TO GET STARTED:

- Do chores around the house naked. Try it first on your own and then with family and friends around.

- While swimming, lose your bathing trunks and continue to swim proudly.

- When buying clothes, leave the changing-room curtain open.

- While at a friend's party, do a streak and then take your time to get dressed again.

- Try running naked through the cafeteria at school, university or work.

- Streak at a football, cricket or rugby match. Most sporting events will do.

- On quiet evenings, walk home from the pub naked. (NB. Take a backpack.)

TIPS FOR THE
ASPIRING DICK-TRICKER

THE ICE-BREAKER

Before exposing yourself to the audience, explain the art form you are about to perform, then show them the Ice-breaker. This involves simply revealing your flaccid penis.

Most people will initially find this shocking, so it's important to let them have a good long look. Once the shock factor is out of the way you can get on with the serious business of genital origami.

INTRODUCING TRICKS

It is very important to introduce the tricks in an energetic and articulate manner, as this will be a huge part of your performance. Think of something witty and descriptive to say, but don't get too cocky, remember that you are extremely vulnerable to criticism while naked.

It is also important to use a 'reveal technique' while presenting your art. For example, with your back to your intended audience say, 'Ladies and gentlemen, please sink your teeth into' – turn to reveal installation – 'a Hamburger!'

HELPFUL HINTS FOR
GENITAL ORIGAMI

1. Because many people in the world still have a problem with seeing naked male genitals it is most important to make sure your audience is willing and accepting of this art form. Genital origami is not designed to shock or offend.

2. This art comes from a tropical climate, so beware of performing in cold conditions; this can cause shrinkage and much embarrassment.

3. In the West, drugs and alcohol are very popular with the young, but they do nothing to enhance the art of genital origami. They might do wonders for the confidence, but they will stifle your capabilities.

4. Your hands are the vehicles of this art, so it is most important to ensure that they are clean and free of toxins, e.g., chillies.

5. The art is strong, but the man is weak, so avoid eye contact with those you find attractive while performing.

WARM-UP TRICKS

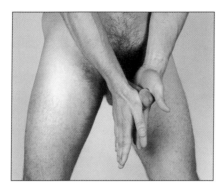

START A FIRE

Rub penis vigorously between the palms of both hands.

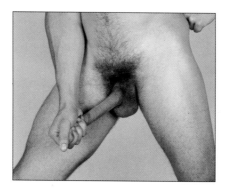

WIND-UP

Take the head of the penis, stretch and then wind
in a circular motion.

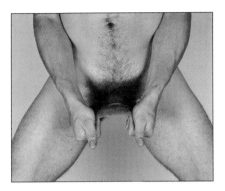

PARACHUTE

Grip the corners of the scrotum with both hands
and pull outwards.

INDEX OF TRICKS
(IN ORDER OF DIFFICULTY)

WOMAN

1. Grasp the head of the penis.

2. Pull the penis back up between the legs and clench it firmly between the butt cheeks.

GET IN TOUCH WITH YOUR FEMININE SIDE.

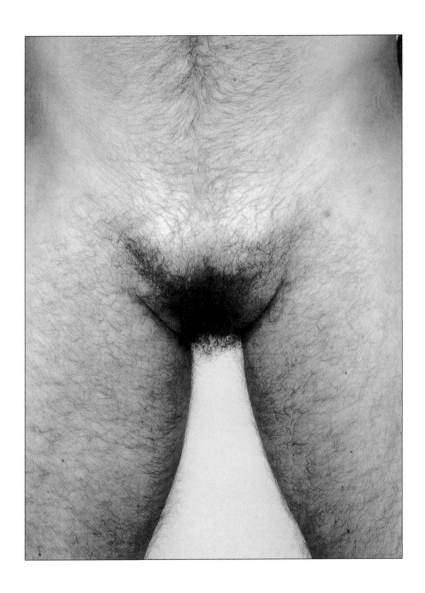

UMBILICAL CORD

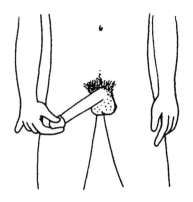

1. Grasp the head of the penis and draw skyward at full stretch.

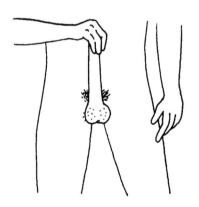

2. Place penis head over belly button.

IF YOUR BELLY BUTTON IS 'TOO HIGH' LEAN FORWARD.

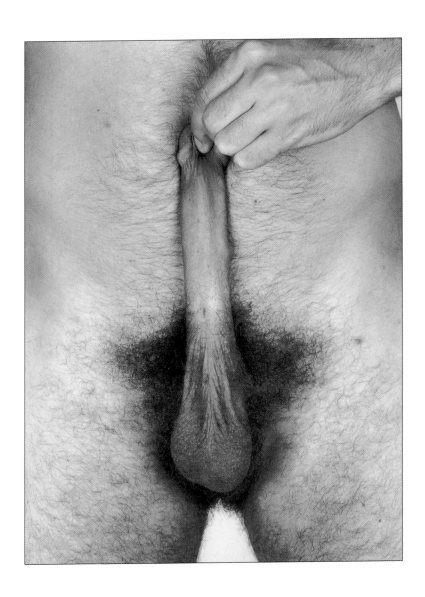

BULLDOG

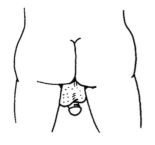

1. With your back turned, stand in the A-frame position.

2. Reach around the back with your preferred hand and gently grasp the testicles, holding the penis from the front with the other hand.

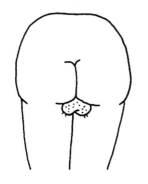

3. Bring your legs together so that only the testicles are visible from behind.

WOOF WOOF!

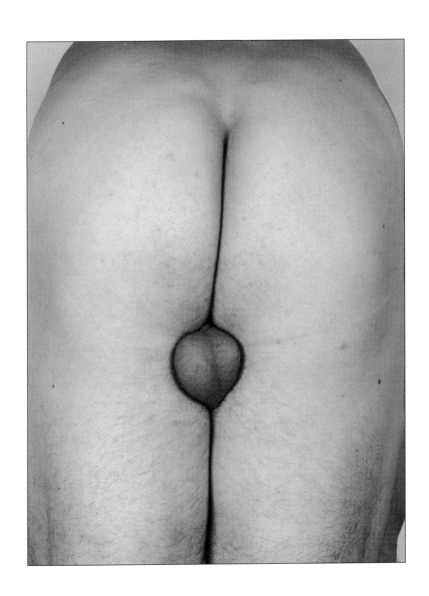

SWOLLEN THUMB

1. Hide your thumb in the palm of your hand and display four fingers.

2. Place the hand next to the penis so it represents the thumb.

NOT ONE FOR HITCH-HIKING.

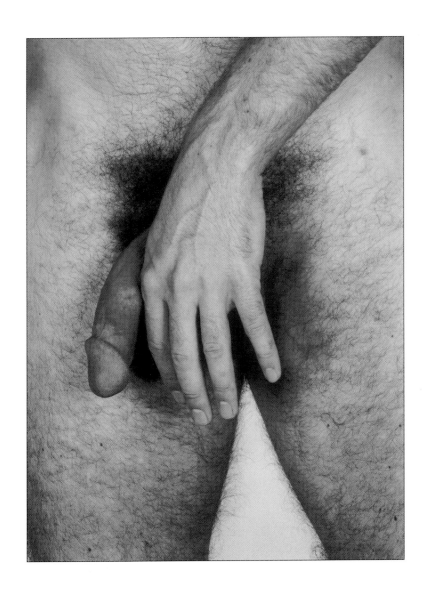

WEDDING RING

1. With your right hand, grasp the penis and place it between the ring and small finger of your outstretched left hand, with your palm facing your body.

2. Wrap the penis around your ring finger, close to the knuckle, and secure the penis between your fingers.

DON'T USE THIS ONE AT THE ALTAR, GUYS!

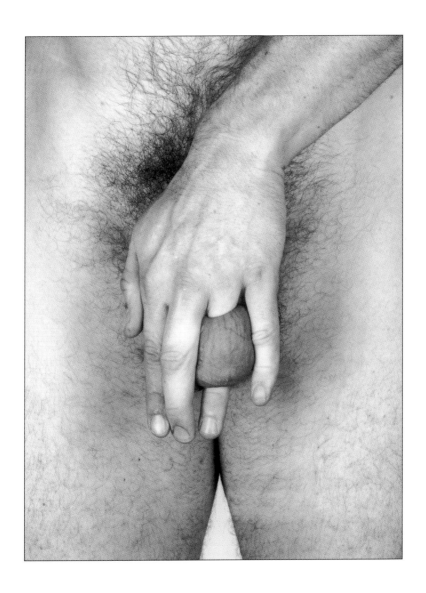

WRISTWATCH

1. Take the head of the penis in your right hand.

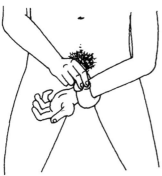

2. Place it inside the left wrist.

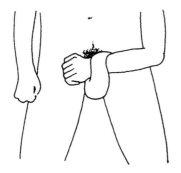

3. Roll the wrist towards your body.

GOT THE TIME?

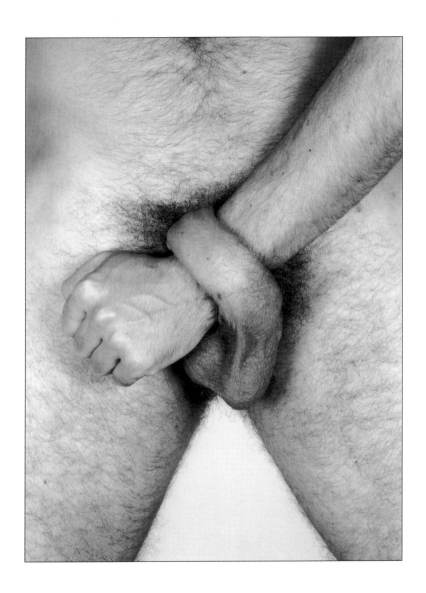

BRAIN

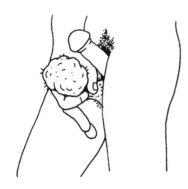

1. Encircle the testicles with
   your thumb and forefinger.

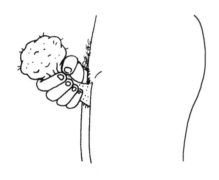

2. Draw the testicles skywards
   and clasp tightly.

**THE THINKING
MAN'S DICK TRICK.**

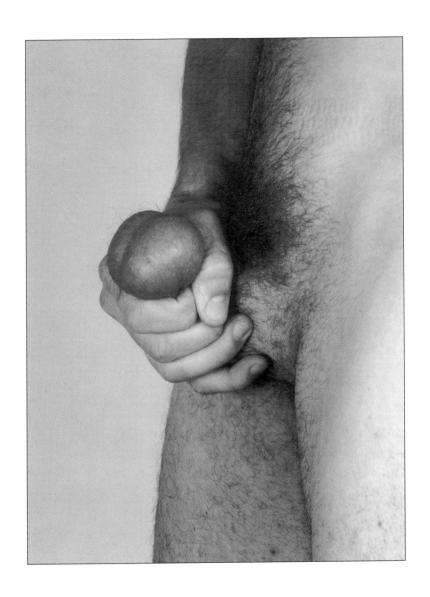

EYE

1. Pinch the skin just below the head of the penis with both thumb and forefinger.

2. Pop the head of the penis back inside the skin.

3. Tug slightly on the skin to create the eyelid.

A WINK'S AS GOOD AS A NOD.

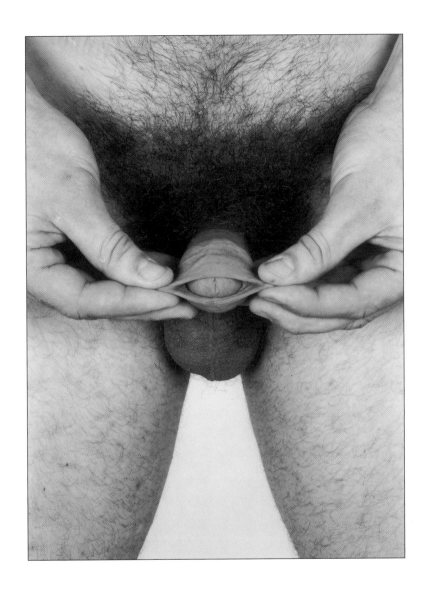

EIFFEL TOWER

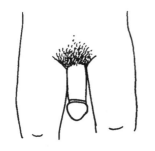

1. Stand in the A-frame position.

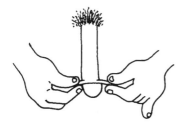

2. Pinch the skin just below the head of the penis with the thumb and forefinger of both hands.

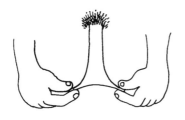

3. Stretch downwards and outwards so the skin covers the head of the penis.

VOILÀ! FRANCE'S MOST FAMOUS LANDMARK.

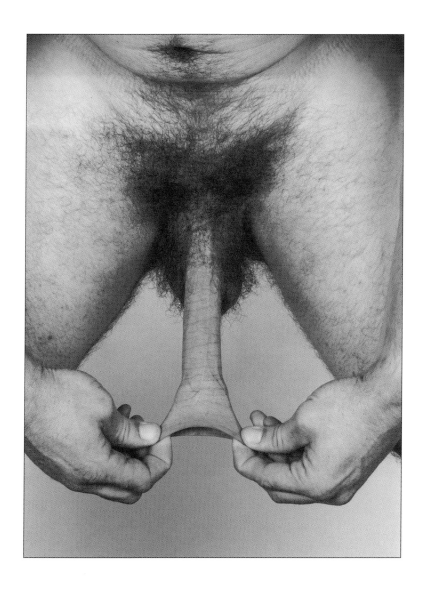

BOOMERANG

1. Remove the testicles from the scrotum

2. Grasp and cover the head of the penis with one hand, and with the other hold the base of the scrotum.

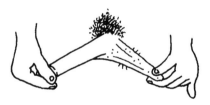

3. Pull down with both hands at a 45-degree angle to form an upside-down V.

THIS ONE WILL ALWAYS COME BACK.

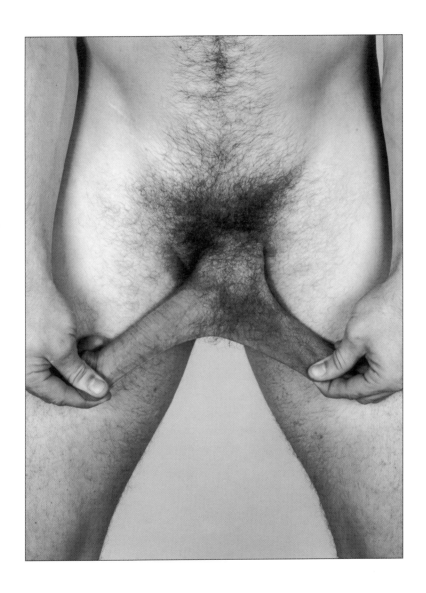

WINDSURFER

1. Stretch the scrotum outwards, holding the furthest corner.

2. Hold the head of the penis with the other hand.

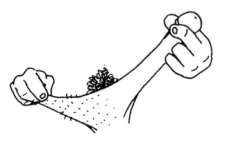

3. Pull the penis skyward while stretching out the scrotum.

ONE FOR BEACH BUMS EVERYWHERE.

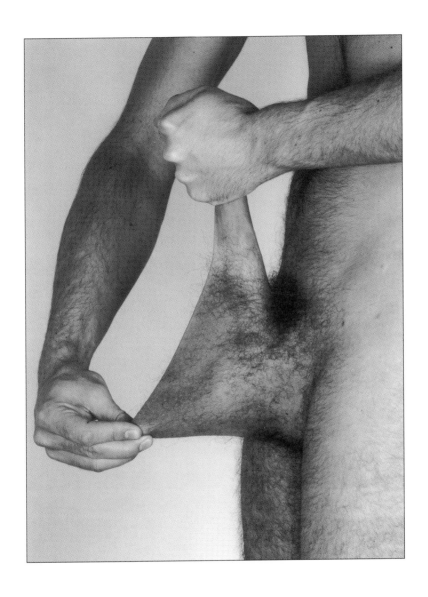

BABY BIRD

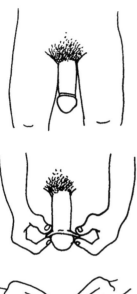

1. Stand in the A-frame position.

2. Using the thumb and forefinger of both hands, pinch the skin just below the head of the penis.

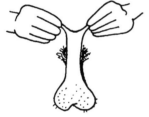

3. Stretch skywards and outwards so the skin covers the head of the penis.

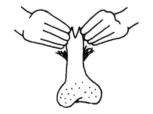

4. Open and close while whistling like a bird.

THE CUTEST DICK TRICK, AND A SPRINGTIME FAVOURITE.

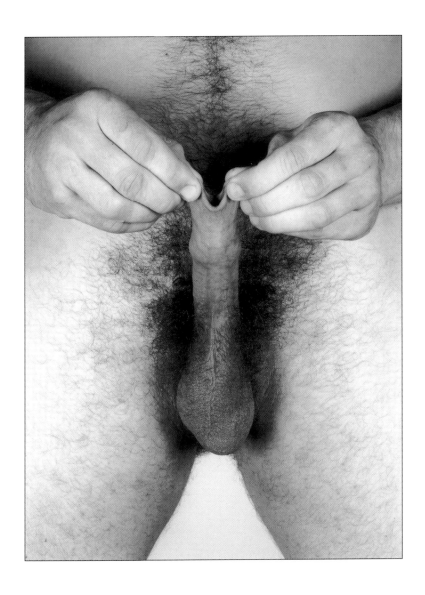

TURTLE

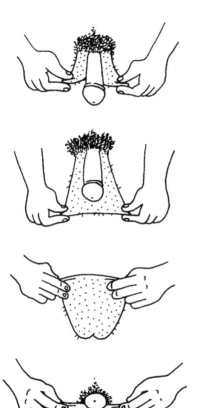

1. Grasp the scrotum at the front of the testicles with both hands.

2. Pull downwards so the scrotum is below the head of the dangling penis.

3. Draw skywards and hold the scrotum against the body, encasing the penis*.

4. Very slowly move both hands downwards in alignment with the body to reveal the head of the penis. Continue moving downwards until the whole penis emerges from the shell.

THIS TRICK ALSO MAKES GOOD SOUP.

*This move is also known as the Last Chicken in the Shop.

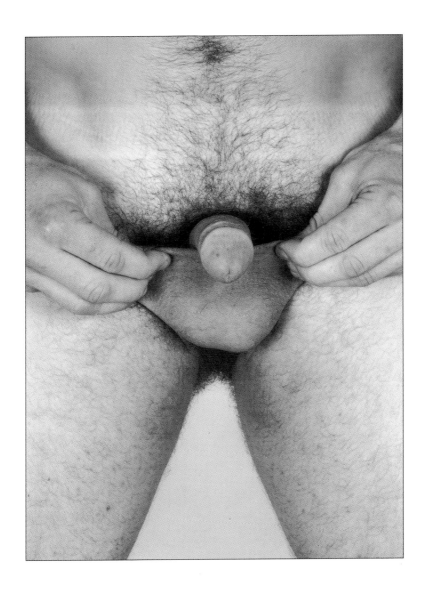

HAIRY TONGUE

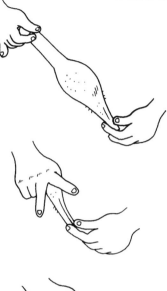

1. Remove the testicles from the scrotum.

2. Grasp the base of the scrotum with your right hand and pull downwards through the forefinger and middle finger of your left hand.

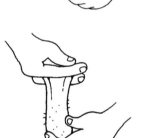

3. Close the fore and middle fingers of your left hand and pull the entire scrotum downwards.

4. Release the scrotum with your right hand and flick it like a licking tongue.

THE CROWDS WILL LAP THIS ONE UP.

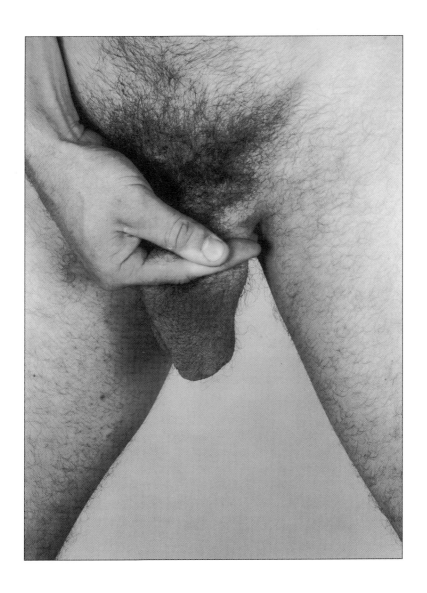

51

PELICAN

1. Pull the penis sideways with one hand.

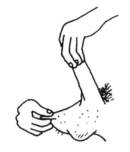

2. With the other hand, pinch the corner of the scrotum and stretch it to the head of the penis.

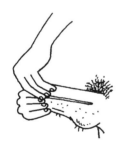

3. Begin snapping at a 90-degree angle.

ITS BEAK CAN HOLD MORE THAN ITS BELLY CAN.

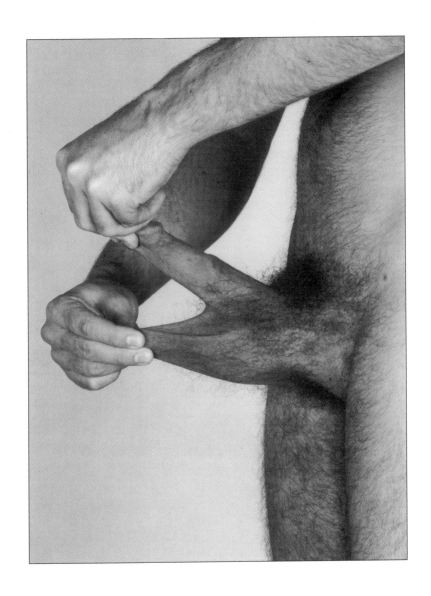

ULURU (AYERS ROCK)

1. Pull down the corners of the scrotum with both hands.

2. Pull the scrotum up over the penis.

3. Tuck the testicles into position and squeeze into the shape of Uluru, then recline.

ALWAYS A TOURIST ATTRACTION.

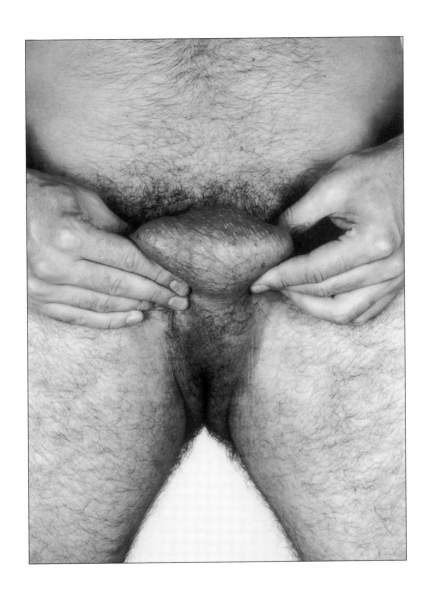

ATOMIC MUSHROOM

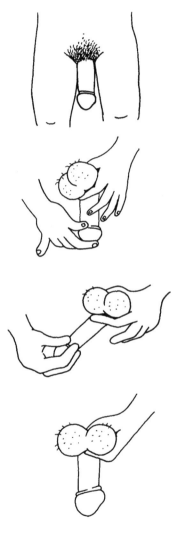

1. Stand in the A-frame position.

2. Loosely hold the penis with one hand while encircling the testicles with the thumb and forefinger of the other hand.

3. Roll the testicles onto the base of the penis.

4. Encircling both the testicles and penis, squeeze and hold with one hand.

EAT YOUR HEART OUT, GONZO.

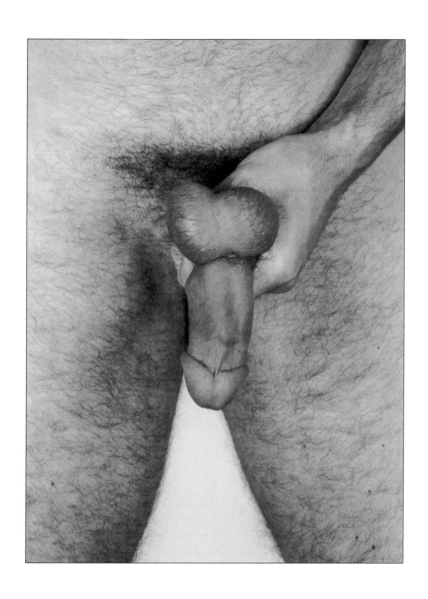

SNAIL

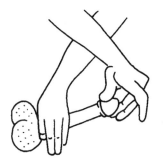

1. Encircle the testicles with the thumb and forefinger of one hand, and with the other hold the head of the penis.

2. Pull the testicles on top of the base of the penis.

3. Tuck the testicles firmly over the penis.

**THERE'S NOTHING
SLOW ABOUT
THIS TRICK.**

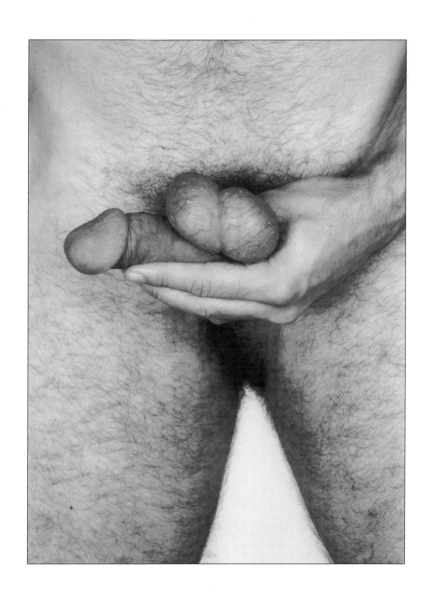

JOEY IN THE POUCH

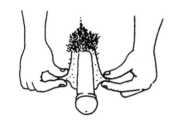

1. Grasp the scrotum at the front of the testicles with both hands.

2. Pull to the sides so the base of the scrotum forms a parallel line with the head of the penis.

3. Draw the scrotum skywards and hold it tightly against the body, so the head of the penis is still displayed.

4. Using both middle fingers, move the testicles up and down to resemble the legs of a baby kangaroo kicking inside the pouch.

AUSTRALIA'S MOST FAMOUS ANIMAL.

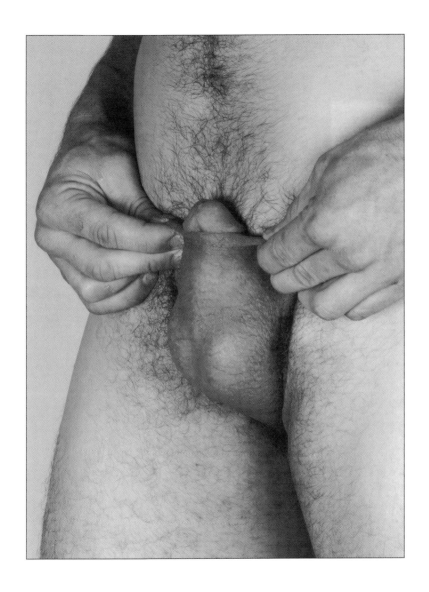

HOT DOG

1. Place the testicles on your fingertips.

2. Fold the testicles up over the penis.

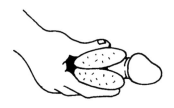

3. Hold like a hot dog.

A TASTY TREAT.

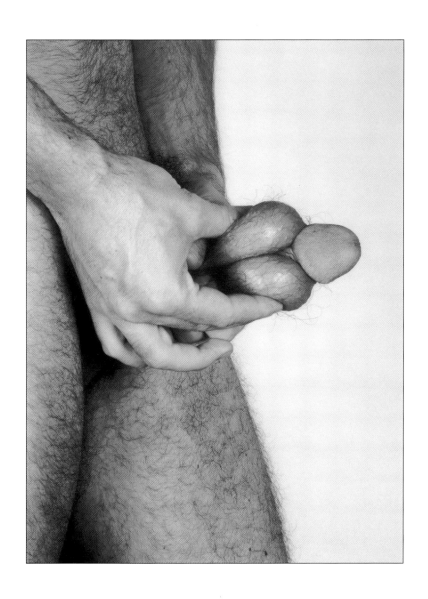

SOUTHERN FRIED CHICKEN

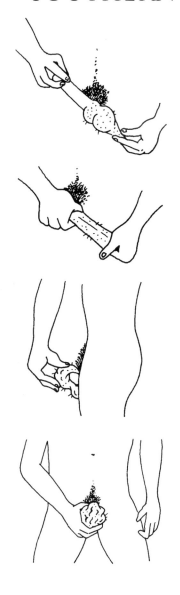

1. Remove the testicles from the scrotum.

2. Tightly encircle the scrotum as close as possible to the body with your thumb and forefinger, pulling the excess scrotum skin with your free hand.

3. Spread the scrotum skin over your fist.

4. Release the scrotum skin to form the shape of southern fried chicken.

FINGER-LICKING GOOD.

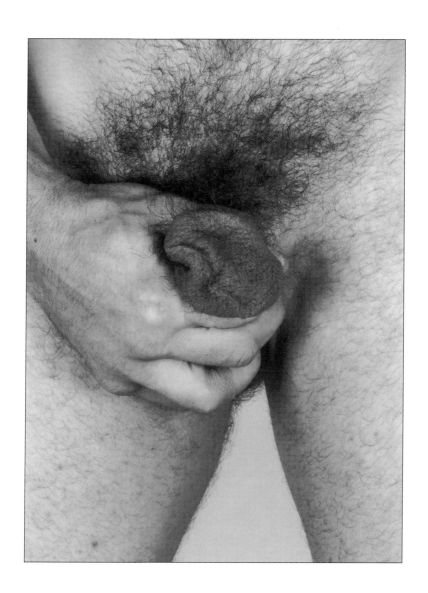

HAMBURGER

1. Place the testicles on your fingertips.

2. Roll the penis between the testicles.

3. Turn on a 90-degree angle.

4. Squeeze the testicles and hold like a hamburger.

WOULD YOU LIKE FRIES WITH THAT?

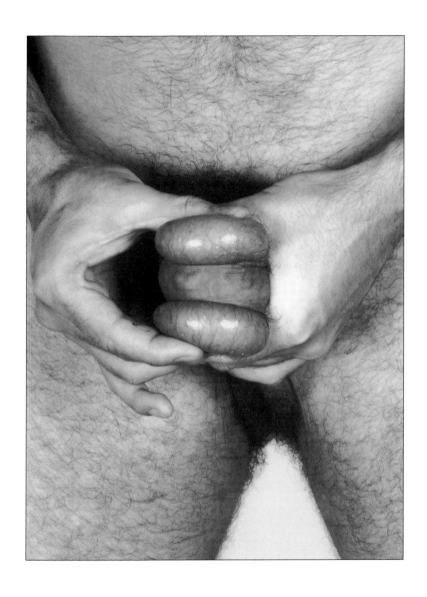

EMU

1. Take the head of the penis with one hand and raise it skywards.

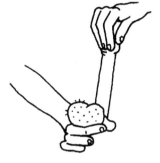

2. Encircle the testicles and base of the penis with your thumb and forefinger.

3. Squeeze until the testicles bulge, then pinch the penis just below the head.

THIS ONE WILL RUN AND RUN.

OTHER WOMAN

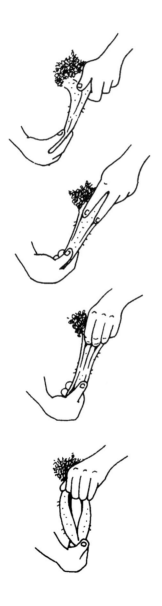

1. Remove the testicles from the scrotum.

2. Using both hands, hold the top and bottom of the scrotum and stretch vertically.

3. Using two fingers, create two crevasses running down the scrotum.

4. Pull the scrotum back between the legs.

DON'T TRY THIS ON A FIRST DATE.

LOCH NESS MONSTER

1. Grasp the head of the penis with one hand and pull sideways. With the other hand, hold the testicles next to each other.

2. Prop up the testicles to create two humps.

3. Pinch the penis below the head and raise skywards. The search is over, Nessy does exist.

TRY THIS ONE IN THE BATH.

SKATEBOARD

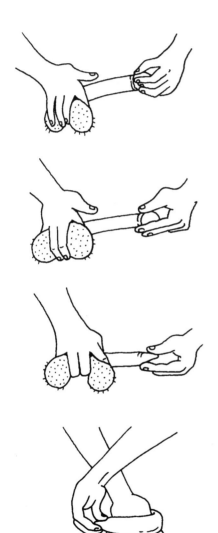

1. Pull the penis to the side with your left hand, and bulge a testicle between two fingers of your right hand.

2. Separate the testicles with two fingers of your right hand.

3. Tuck your fingers up to allow the testicles to hang free.

4. Pull the penis back across the fingers.

A GNARLY DICK TRICK.

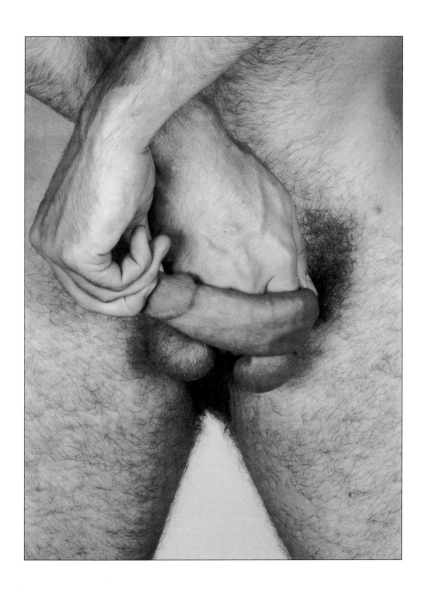

A NOTE FROM THE DOCTOR

Dr I C Perry

5 October 2000

Re: Mr Simon MORLEY & Mr David FRIEND – **'Puppetry of the Penis'.**

As requested, I have examined the above named persons in connection with their stage act.

I am satisfied, that providing my precautions are observed, no long-term damage or injury will result from their theatrical performance.

Yours sincerely

Dr I C Perry
Consultant in Occupational Medicine

THE DOCTOR

ACKNOWLEDGEMENTS
(IN NO SPECIFIC ORDER)

Alan Length, Dr Rob McInnes, Mel Zimmek, Tucky and the Corner Hotel, Matt and Penny Everett, Tony Martin, Mick Molloy, Andrew Denton, James Penlidis, Razuki family, Dean and Jamie Duursma, The Burwood Mutants, Nicko and Buff Farnell (The Australian Dick Trickers Association), Janey Rainey, Jimeoin, Steve Curry, Simon Pendergast, Dave and Toby, Nick and Sarah, Charlie and Dawn Chow, Adrian Chow, Mick Burns, Austereo, JJJ, Nigel LaBrooy, The Gold Rats of Lismore, The Butler St Boys, Richard Temple, David Johnson, Clare Conville, Tim Fountain, Cookie Crowder, Glen Robbins, Etnies, Rooster Molloy, Dr Vanitha (Gina), Arnette, James Young, David Vodica, 3RRR, Carolyn and Tim Friend, Paul Dumais, Penny Gardner, Fred Negro, Matt Mylecharane, Patrick Walsh, Johnny Ring, Patrick Janson-Smith, Shauna Bartlett, Lucy Bennett, Alison Martin and Aelred Doyle.

And especially Darren Chow, the third member of *Puppetry of the Penis*, 'not just a cameraman!'

HEALTH WARNING

Excessive practising of genital origami may result in irreparable harm. Failure to take note of this will result in what your mothers always told you would happen...

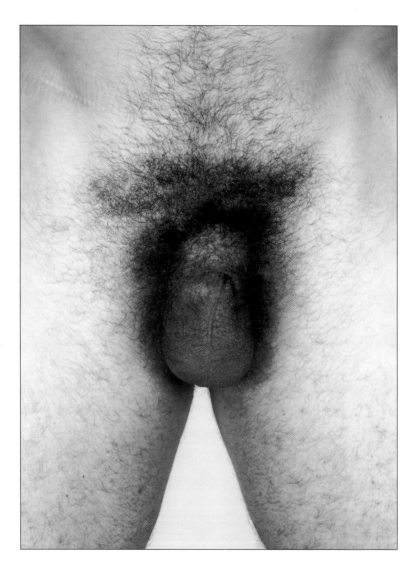

NO DICK